Challenger Writing
SECOND EDITION
ADULT READING SERIES

Skill-building writing exercises

for each lesson in *Challenger 3* of the

Challenger Adult Reading Series

McVey & Associates, Inc.

New Readers Press

Challenger Writing 3, 2nd Edition
ISBN 978-1-56420-902-3

Copyright © 2010, 1994 New Readers Press
New Readers Press
A Publishing Division of ProLiteracy
1320 Jamesville Avenue, Syracuse, New York 13210
www.newreaderspress.com

All rights reserved. No part of this book may be reproduced or transmitted in any form or by any means, electronic or mechanical, including photocopying, recording, or by any information storage and retrieval system, without permission in writing from the publisher.

Printed in the United States of America
9 8 7 6 5 4 3

All proceeds from the sale of New Readers Press materials support literacy programs in the United States and worldwide.

Developmental Editor: Terrie Lipke
Contributing Writer: Practical Strategies, Inc.
Creative Director: Andrea Woodbury
Production Specialist: Maryellen Casey
Cover Design: Carolyn Wallace

Contents

Lesson 1 4
Lesson 2 6
Lesson 3 8
Lesson 4 10
Lesson 5 12
Lesson 6 14
Lesson 7 16
Lesson 8 18
Lesson 9 20
Lesson 10 22
Lesson 11 24
Lesson 12 26
Lesson 13 28
Lesson 14 30
Lesson 15 32
Lesson 16 34
Lesson 17 36
Lesson 18 38
Lesson 19 40
Lesson 20 42
Review 44

Lesson 1

1 Use These Words in Sentences. Use some of the words below to write three sentences that tell something about the story "Steven Takes Some Advice."

| advice | driving | pact | sore | tense |
| business | exercise | rut | temper | visits |

1. _____

2. _____

3. _____

2 What Do You Think? Complete the sentences with words that tell what you think.

1. A job that makes me feel tense is _____

2. When I feel tense and need to relax, I _____

3. Sometimes I lose my temper when _____

4. When I want to exercise, I _____

3 Combine the Sentences. Combine each pair of sentences below to make one sentence.

1. I put the dirty dishes in a dishpan. Then I washed the dishes.

2. Today's newspaper had a story. The story was about a plan that backfired.

3. The sidewalk in front of my house is broken. The city will fix the sidewalk.

4. Many workers use toolboxes. They carry in their toolboxes the tools they need to do their jobs.

4 Complete These Paragraphs. Complete the following paragraphs in your own words.

1. Steven's sister Ruth told him he should go out more, do things, and meet some new people. I think Ruth's advice was _____

2. People who sit a lot at their jobs can get stiff and sore. Some things they can do to feel better are _____

Lesson 1

Lesson 2

1 Use These Words in Sentences. Use some of the words below to write three sentences that tell something about the story "Meet Jerome."

| confused | exercise | peaceful | splurge | stunt |
| crazy | mistake | perched | stew | yoga |

1. _____

2. _____

3. _____

2 What Do You Think? Complete the sentences with words that tell what you think.

1. If I saw a friend standing on his head, I would think _____

2. I think exercise is good for people because _____

3. One good change I could make in my life is _____

4. Classes can help people _____

3 Put These Sentences in Order. Write these sentences in the correct time order on the lines below.

Jerome was feasting on beef stew.

Steven treated Jerome to a steak dinner.

Steven was standing on his head.

Jerome said he did not think Steven was crazy.

1. _____
2. _____
3. _____
4. _____

4 Complete These Paragraphs. Complete the following paragraphs in your own words.

1. Steven took a yoga class by mistake. He couldn't tell Jerome the difference between a yoga class and an exercise class because _____

_____

_____

_____

_____

2. Steven was standing on his head in the middle of his bedroom. His face had a very peaceful look because he _____

_____

_____

_____

_____

3. Steven cared what Jerome thought because Jerome was his best friend. Steven was glad Jerome did not laugh at him, so he _____

_____

_____

_____

_____

Lesson 3

1 Use These Words in Sentences. Use some of the words below to write three sentences that tell something about the story "Jerome Learns About Yoga."

| balance | flip | Internet | scrolled | shoulder | yoga |
| figure | frightened | muscles | search | website | |

1. _____

2. _____

3. _____

2 What Do You Think? Complete the sentences with words that tell what you think.

1. There are many ways to learn new things. Three ways to learn new things are _____

2. Yoga helps with balance and helps people relax. I might try yoga if _____

3 Combine the Sentences. Combine each pair of sentences below to make one sentence.

1. Divers use flashlights. They use flashlights to see in deep water.
   _____
   _____

2. You can use these folders. Your reports can be filed in these folders.
   _____
   _____

3. Students use notebooks. They use notebooks to write down important information.
   _____
   _____

4. Swimmers use towels. Swimmers need to dry off when they come out of a pool.
   _____
   _____

5. People use mats in yoga class. They sit or lie on the mats to do moves.
   _____
   _____

4 Complete These Paragraphs. Complete the following paragraphs in your own words.

1. Jerome thought it would be easy to stand on his head. He found out that _____
   _____
   _____

2. Jerome thought Steven should stop taking yoga lessons. He wanted to talk Steven out of going to yoga classes, but first he _____
   _____
   _____

Lesson 3

Lesson 4

1 Use These Words in Sentences. Use some of the words below to write three sentences that tell something about the story "Ginger Is Grumpy."

| Ginger | grudge | hung up | relax | stress |
| grouchy | headache | pigpen | screaming | yoga |

1. _____

2. _____

3. _____

2 What Do You Think? Complete the answers to the questions with words that tell what you think.

1. How do you get along with a grouchy person? I get along with a grouchy person by _____

2. What kinds of things make you feel better when you feel grouchy? Things that make me feel better are _____

3 Put These Sentences in Order. Write these sentences in the correct time order on the lines below.

"I always come over to your place," complained Jerome.

Ginger let the phone ring a few times before she picked it up.

Jerome yelled at Ginger to stop screaming.

Ginger asked Jerome if he was coming over.

1. _____
2. _____
3. _____
4. _____

4 Complete These Paragraphs. Complete the following paragraphs in your own words.

1. Jerome started to explain yoga to Ginger, but he ended up being rude to her. She _____
_____
_____
_____
_____

2. Jerome started to stick up for himself. He _____
_____
_____
_____
_____

3. When someone is rude to me, I _____
_____
_____
_____
_____

Lesson 5

1 Use These Words in Sentences. Use some of the words below to write three sentences that tell something about the story "Who Is Ginger?"

| bank | homey | lessons | owned | singer | thrift |
| hardware | land | money | saved | store | truthful |

1. _____

2. _____

3. _____

2 What Do You Think? Complete the answers to the questions with words that tell what you think.

1. Why do you think Ginger doesn't spend much money on her home? I think Ginger doesn't spend much because _____

2. Do you think you could be as thrifty as Ginger? I think _____

3 Combine the Sentences. Combine each pair of sentences below to make one sentence.

1. Anne was madly in love. She was in love with Ben and wanted to marry him.

2. The boxer swung wildly. He slipped and fell against the ropes.

3. John had been away a lot lately. We hadn't seen him for a while.

4 Complete These Paragraphs. Complete the following paragraphs in your own words.

1. Ginger's grandmother helped her learn about thrift. I know Ginger was thrifty because she ____

2. I think saving money is smart. I would like to save a lot, but sometimes I ____

3. I want to save money for certain things. I'd like ____

Lesson 5 13

Lesson 6

1 Use These Words in Sentences. Use some of the words below to write three sentences that tell something about the story "A Strange Twist of Fate."

| apartment | fingers | mess | paint | snatch | Tony |
| counter | loose | oozing | paycheck | tilted | wiped |

1. _____

2. _____

3. _____

2 What Do You Think? Complete the answers to the questions with words that tell what you think.

1. Why did Jerome reach for the can of blue paint? Jerome reached for the can of blue paint because _____

2. Why do you think it took seven hours to clean up the mess? I think it took seven hours to clean up the mess because _____

3 Put These Sentences in Order. Write these sentences in the correct time order on the lines below.

Tony laughed so hard that he nearly slipped on the paint.

Jerome reached for the can.

Jerome thought about snatching a can of blue paint.

Five gallons of blue paint poured over him.

1. _____
2. _____
3. _____
4. _____

4 Complete These Paragraphs. Complete the following paragraphs in your own words.

1. Jerome thought about snatching the paint and paying for it out of his next week's paycheck. If he did that, Jerome might have a problem because _____
_____
_____
_____

2. Jerome thought about giving Ginger a gift of paint so that she would talk to him again. Giving gifts to people when they are angry at you is _____
_____
_____
_____

3. Spilled paint makes a huge mess that is hard to clean off papers and clothes. Other things that make a mess are _____
_____
_____
_____

Lesson 6

Lesson 7

1 Use These Words in Sentences. Use some of the words below to write three sentences that tell something about the story "At Yoga Class."

| certain | coffee | exercises | knack | restless | sugar |
| chocolate | cold | involved | nasty | stress | unhealthy |

1. _____

2. _____

3. _____

2 What Do You Think? Answer these questions in complete sentences that tell what you think.

1. Steven forgot about his cold during the yoga class. Do you feel better when you exercise? Why or why not?

   _____

2. People eat many kinds of foods. Which foods that you eat are healthy for you? Which are unhealthy?

   _____

3 Combine the Sentences. Combine each set of sentences below to make one sentence.

1. Steven had a cold. He didn't feel well. Steven went to his yoga class anyway.

   _____
   _____

2. Holly told Steven he should not eat sugar. She said sugar makes people grouchy. She said it makes them restless, too.

   _____
   _____

3. Holly went to the yoga class for exercise. She also went to the class because it made her feel peaceful. Yoga made her more relaxed.

   _____
   _____

4 Write a Paragraph. Write a short paragraph about making your life more healthy. Use the questions below to guide you.

Do you eat foods that are good for you?

What foods could you eat that would be better for you?

Do you get enough exercise?

What new exercise could you do that would be good for you?

How could your life be better if you ate better food and got more exercise?

_____
_____
_____
_____
_____
_____
_____
_____

Lesson 8

1 Use These Words in Sentences. Use some of the words below to write three sentences that tell something about the story "Ginger Gives Some Advice."

bragging	expect	greed	proud	temper
bruises	folks	mailman	slouched	think about

1. _____

2. _____

3. _____

2 What Do You Think? Answer these questions in complete sentences that tell what you think.

1. Gail went to Ginger's apartment because she didn't want to be alone. Do you think Gail also thought Ginger could help her? How?

   _____

2. Gail said her father gets angry when she drops by his house. How did Ginger help Gail understand her father's anger?

   _____

3 Put These Sentences in Order. Write these sentences in the correct time order on the lines below.

"You know very well your father's proud of his job," said Ginger.

Gail slouched against Ginger's doorway.

"Go wash your face, and I'll fix you some breakfast," Ginger said.

"My father lost his temper," Gail said.

"Is it okay if I stay here for a day or two?" asked Gail.

1. _____
2. _____
3. _____
4. _____
5. _____

4 Write a Paragraph. Write a short paragraph about giving advice to friends. Use the questions below to guide you.

What kinds of advice do you sometimes give your friends?

When do you give advice to your friends?

Are there times when you decide not to give advice? Give an example.

Are you sometimes able to help a friend think of new ways to look at things?

How does your advice help your friends with their problems?

_____
_____
_____
_____
_____
_____
_____
_____

Lesson 8

Lesson 9

1 Use These Words in Sentences. Use some of the words below to write three sentences that tell something about the story "Jerome Gets an E-Card"

| avoid | e-card | goodies | lousy | online | pout |
| cookbook | e-mail | invited | loyal | party | voice mail |

1. _____
   _____

2. _____
   _____

3. _____
   _____

2 What Do You Think? Answer these questions in complete sentences that tell what you think.

1. Jerome had not seen Ginger for four weeks. Do you think Jerome should have called Ginger? Why or why not?
   _____
   _____
   _____
   _____

2. Jerome had made fun of Steven's yoga class. Why do you think he had done this?
   _____
   _____
   _____
   _____

3 Combine the Sentences. Combine each set of sentences below to make one sentence.

1. The beef was frozen. I left it out to thaw. Then I used it to make a stew.

2. Ginger has written a book. The book is a health food cookbook. The book is selling well.

3. Joyce stopped to loosen the straps. The straps were too tight. The straps were on her backpack.

4 Write a Paragraph. Write a short paragraph about the way to treat friends. Use the questions below to guide you.

Would you try to help a friend who is feeling sad? Why or why not?

What might you do to help a friend who is feeling sad?

Would you expect your friend to do anything for you in return?

How would you expect to feel after helping a friend?

Lesson 10

1 Use These Words in Sentences. Use some of the words below to write three sentences that tell something about the story "Jerome Goes to the Laundromat."

| clothes | jerk | losing | quarters | search | straightened out |
| fault | laundromat | machines | remember | slot | |

1. _____

2. _____

3. _____

2 What Do You Think? Answer these questions in complete sentences that tell what you think.

1. Jerome didn't like going to the laundromat. How do you feel about going to laundromats?

_____

2. Holly told Jerome he was a jerk. Do you agree? Why or why not?

_____

3 Put These Sentences in Order. Write these sentences in the correct time order on the lines below.

Jerome found Holly at the laundromat.

Jerome said women stick together like glue.

Holly said that Jerome is a jerk.

Jerome told Holly that Ginger should say she is sorry.

Jerome threw his laundry in the trunk of his car.

1. _____
2. _____
3. _____
4. _____
5. _____

4 Write a Paragraph. Write a short paragraph about doing laundry. Use the questions below to guide you.

Do you do your own laundry or does someone else do it for you?

Are your clothes washed at your home or at a laundromat?

Are your clothes dried in a machine or are they hung up to dry?

Who folds and puts your clothes away?

Is this the best way to do your laundry or is there a better way?

_____
_____
_____
_____
_____
_____
_____

Lesson 11

1 Use These Words in Sentences. Use some of the words below to write three sentences that tell something about the story "The Camping Trip."

| berserk | daydreaming | hiked | nervous | path | spied |
| camping | growling | listen | newspaper | phone | wild animal |

1. _____

2. _____

3. _____

2 What Do You Think? Answer these questions in complete sentences that tell what you think.

1. Do you think Ginger would be scared to camp alone again?

2. Why do you think the fishermen might have thought Ginger was nuts?

3. Why did Ginger say she would carry her cell phone everywhere, paint all the walls, and read every single newspaper she could find?

3 Combine the Sentences. Combine each set of sentences below to make one sentence.

1. I don't recall my first party. I remember my first dance. I remember my first date.

   _____
   _____

2. Sam often sounds edgy. He sounds that way the first time he talks to a woman. He sounds edgy because women make him nervous.

   _____
   _____

3. Mike doesn't like to brag about things he does well. Mary wants people to know how good Mike is. She boasts for him.

   _____
   _____

4 Write a Paragraph. Write a short paragraph about camping. Use the questions below to guide you.

If you were going camping, what food would you take?

Would you take a tent and a sleeping bag?

What tools would you take with you? Why would you take them?

Would you want to camp alone or with a friend? Why?

_____
_____
_____
_____
_____
_____
_____
_____

Lesson 11

Lesson 12

1 Use These Words in Sentences. Use some of the words below to write three sentences that tell something about the story "Steven's New Game."

| baseball | dance | golf | natural | tennis | video |
| clumsy | excited | movement | sulk | tripped | workout |

1. _____

2. _____

3. _____

2 What Do You Think? Answer these questions in complete sentences that tell what you think.

1. Why was Holly so grumpy at first about playing video games?

   _____

2. Holly told Steven that he would get the hang of the dance game. Why do you think Holly said this?

   _____

3 Put These Sentences in Order. Write these sentences in the correct time order on the lines below.

Steven tripped and missed steps in the dance game.

Steven swung his arms like he was swinging a baseball bat.

Holly said she could play this game all day.

Holly wanted to play a game that was more like yoga.

Steven showed Holly how to swing her arms like she was playing golf.

1. _____
2. _____
3. _____
4. _____
5. _____

4 Write a Paragraph. Write a short paragraph about sports. Use the questions below to guide you.

Why do you like (or not like) to watch certain sports?

Why do you like (or not like) to play certain sports?

Which do you enjoy more, watching sports or playing them? Why?

Have you ever played sports on a video game system?

If so, which sports did you play?

Did you enjoy playing them?

_____
_____
_____
_____
_____
_____
_____

Lesson 13

1 Use These Words in Sentences. Use some of the words below to write three sentences that tell something about the story "Jerome's Scheme."

| apartment | cleaned | gobble | party | scheme | waiting |
| cinch | dancing | indulge | problem | shopping | wreck |

1. _____

2. _____

3. _____

2 What Do You Think? Answer these questions in complete sentences that tell what you think.

1. Jerome thought that getting Ginger to his party would help straighten things out. Do you think it was a good idea? Why or why not?

   _____

2. Jerome threw himself on his couch because he was feeling sorry for himself. Do you think that was a grown-up way to act? Why or why not?

   _____

3 Combine the Sentences. Combine each set of sentences below to make one sentence.

1. Jerome had a scheme. The scheme involved Tony. Ginger was involved in the scheme, too.

_____

_____

2. Jerome bought bug spray. He swept the cobwebs from the ceiling. He scrubbed the carpet.

_____

_____

3. Jerome went online and got hip-hop music. He burned a CD with the songs. He also added some Cuban music for the CD.

_____

_____

4 Write a Paragraph. Write a short paragraph about planning a party. Use the questions below to guide you.

What kind of party do you want to plan?

Who will you invite to the party?

What will you have to eat and drink at the party?

What will you do during the party?

Will everyone have a good time?

_____

_____

_____

_____

_____

_____

_____

_____

Lesson 14

1 Use These Words in Sentences. Use some of the words below to write three sentences that tell something about the story "Whatever Happened to Tony and Ginger?"

| avoided | charges | complain | fought | neighbor |
| buzz saw | chestnut | deed | motel | property |

1. _____

2. _____

3. _____

2 What Do You Think? Answer these questions in complete sentences that tell what you think.

1. If you were Tony, how would you handle the problem over the chestnut tree?

_____

2. How do you think Tony should treat Mrs. Darkpill?

_____

3 Put These Sentences in Order. Write these sentences in the correct time order on the lines below.

Tony heard the sound of a buzz saw.

Mrs. Darkpill called the police.

Mrs. Darkpill complained about the chestnut tree.

Tony yelled at Mrs. Darkpill's kids.

Tony bought a small house.

1. _____
2. _____
3. _____
4. _____
5. _____

4 Write a Paragraph. Write a short paragraph using the questions below to guide you.

Think of someone you know who is like Mrs. Darkpill.

What problems have you or other people had with that person?

How did you or other people handle a problem with that person?

Was that the best way to handle the problem, or were there better ways to handle it?

_____
_____
_____
_____
_____
_____
_____
_____
_____

Lesson 15

1 Use These Words in Sentences. Use some of the words below to write three sentences that tell something about the story "Mrs. Darkpill."

| barged | driveway | fight | keyboard | police |
| cupboard | exciting | frightened | neighbor | tree |

1. _____

2. _____

3. _____

2 What Do You Think? Answer these questions in complete sentences that tell what you think.

1. What do you think Mrs. Darkpill really wanted when she came to Tony's house?
_____

2. Why do you think Tony tried to stop Ginger from talking to Mrs. Darkpill?
_____

3. Do you think Ginger was making fun of Mrs. Darkpill? Explain your answer.
_____

3 Combine the Sentences. Combine each set of sentences below to make one sentence.

1. Gail had a baby girl. The baby was born last month. The baby weighed seven pounds, eleven ounces.

   _____
   _____

2. I take dancing lessons. My lessons last for one hour. I go once a week.

   _____
   _____

3. I went to the store yesterday. I bought one quart of milk. I bought a can of Coke, too.

   _____
   _____

4 Write a Paragraph. Write a short paragraph using the questions below to guide you.

If you had been Tony, how would you have handled Mrs. Darkpill?

Would you have let her come into the house or not?

Would you have tried to talk with her?

Would you have asked Ginger to go to another room while you talked with Mrs. Darkpill?

What would you have done?

_____
_____
_____
_____
_____
_____
_____
_____

Lesson 15

Lesson 16

1 Use These Words in Sentences. Use some of the words below to write three sentences that tell something about the story "Testing Recipes."

| awful | commit | judge | prunes | rules | wisecracks |
| behave | complex | oven | recipe | taste | |

1. _____

2. _____

3. _____

2 What Do You Think? Answer these questions in complete sentences that tell what you think.

1. Holly tore up her recipe card for prune whip. Why do you think she did this?

_____

2. Holly says that Jerome won't do what he should to get what he wants in life. What do you think she means by that? Explain your answer.

_____

3 Combine the Sentences. Combine each set of sentences below to make one sentence.

1. The elbow is a joint in the body. Another is the knee. The wrist is a joint, too.

   _____

   _____

2. We have a new bathroom. The bathroom has a towel rack. It also has a shower.

   _____

   _____

3. Martin is a good bowler. He is on a bowling team. The team bowls every Thursday.

   _____

   _____

4 Write a Paragraph. Write a short paragraph using the questions below to guide you.

Do you think Jerome is right or wrong?

Do you think he should call Ginger now that he knows what really happened?

Why or why not?

_____

_____

_____

_____

_____

_____

_____

_____

_____

_____

_____

_____

Lesson 17

1 Use These Words in Sentences. Use some of the words below to write three sentences that tell something about the story "Tony's Day Off."

| booth | clothing | curtain | dock | pay | sick |
| breakfast | comply | desire | Mr. Dennis | quiet | unfriendly |

1. _____

2. _____

3. _____

2 What Do You Think? Answer these questions in complete sentences that tell what you think.

1. Why do you think Tony wanted to call in sick?

2. Why did Tony want to tell his boss off?

3. What should Tony have done that day? Explain your answer.

3 Put These Sentences in Order. Write these sentences in the correct time order on the lines below.

Tony chose two pairs of slacks to try on.

Mr. Dennis fired Tony.

Tony went to the clothing sale at the men's store.

Tony shut off the alarm.

Tony told the person in the fitting booth to hurry up.

Tony told Mr. Dennis he was sick.

1. _____
2. _____
3. _____
4. _____
5. _____
6. _____

4 Write a Paragraph. Write a short paragraph using the questions below to guide you.

Do you think it is right or wrong to call in sick when you are not really sick?

Are there times when you think it is all right and other times when it is wrong?

Do you think it hurts anybody else when you are not there?

Give reasons for your answers.

_____
_____
_____
_____
_____
_____
_____

Lesson 17

Lesson 18

1 Use These Words in Sentences. Use some of the words below to write three sentences that tell something about the story "A Talk with Jerome."

| complaining | disgusted | garbage | limit | straightened out |
| disagree | exhausted | important | mistake | upset |

1. _____

2. _____

3. _____

2 What Do You Think? Answer these questions in complete sentences that tell what you think.

1. Jerome felt Steven was being too harsh with him. Why do you think Jerome felt this way?

_____

2. Steven said Jerome should take a chance and call Ginger. Do you agree? Why or why not?

_____

3 Combine the Sentences. Combine each set of sentences below to make one sentence.

1. The carpenter needed some nails. She needed a saw. She had a drill.

2. A fisherman uses a rod for fishing. He uses hooks with the rod. He uses bait, also.

3. A baker uses a rolling pin. The rolling pin is used to roll out dough. The dough is put in pie plates.

4 Write a Paragraph. Write a short paragraph using the questions below to guide you.

Do you think Steven's advice to Jerome was good or bad? Why?

What might Steven have done differently?

What would you have said to Jerome?

Lesson 19

1 Use These Words in Sentences. Use some of the words below to write three sentences that tell something about the story "Jerome and Ginger."

| balcony | downhearted | explain | murmured | sing | upscale |
| café | downhill | lovely | overcome | threatened | |

1. _____

2. _____

3. _____

2 What Do You Think? Answer these questions in complete sentences that tell what you think.

1. Jerome didn't feel downhearted after he decided to act. Why do you think deciding to act helps people feel better?

   _____

2. How have you confronted a problem with another person in your life?

   _____

3 Put These Sentences in Order. Write these sentences in the correct time order on the lines below.

Ginger was angry and turned to walk away.

Jerome decided to see Ginger in person.

Ginger felt Jerome's stare and looked up.

Ginger said she would sing "September Song."

Jerome said he missed Ginger very much.

Jerome went to the club where Ginger was singing.

1. _____
2. _____
3. _____
4. _____
5. _____
6. _____

4 Write a Paragraph. Write a short paragraph using the questions below to guide you.

At first, Jerome made up a story about why he went to the club where Ginger was singing. Can you think of a better way for Jerome to have acted?

Do you think most people would do what Jerome did? Why or why not?

_____
_____
_____
_____
_____
_____
_____
_____
_____

Lesson 20

1 Use These Words in Sentences. Use some of the words below to write three sentences that tell something about the story "Holly's Book Party."

| bookstores | chocolate | cookbook | Holly | recipe | success |
| cheesecake | contract | dessert | honor | spaghetti | |

1. _____

2. _____

3. _____

2 What Do You Think? Answer these questions in complete sentences that tell what you think.

1. Why do you think Jerome calls things like spaghetti "real food"?

_____

2. Why do you think Holly's party was a great success?

_____

3 Combine the Sentences. Combine each set of sentences below to make one sentence.

1. Ben likes to cook. He likes to cook spaghetti. He likes to cook cheesecake, too.

_____

_____

2. I like to play sports. I like baseball. My favorite sport to play is tennis.

_____

_____

3. I carry heavy gear for camping. I use a knapsack for my gear. I carry the knapsack on my back.

_____

_____

4 Write a Paragraph. Write a short paragraph using the questions below to guide you. Explain your answers.

How do you think Jerome's and Ginger's lives will turn out?

Do you think they will stay together for a long time?

Do you think they will be happy together?

Do you think they will talk with each other when they have problems instead of getting angry and not speaking?

_____

_____

_____

_____

_____

_____

_____

_____

Review

1 Combine the Sentences. Combine each pair of sentences below to make one sentence.

1. Ginger finally painted her apartment. She painted it blue. She hung new curtains, too.
   _____
   _____

2. Steven practiced yoga every day. He got very good at yoga. He became a yoga instructor.
   _____
   _____

3. Holly got food from the refrigerator. She cooked the food and ate her dinner. She did all of this in thirty minutes.
   _____
   _____

2 What Do You Think? Answer these questions in complete sentences that tell what you think.

1. Many people like to play or watch basketball. Others don't like it. Do you like the sport of basketball? Why or why not?
   _____
   _____
   _____

2. We are told that exercising is healthy. Do you agree or disagree? Why?
   _____
   _____
   _____

3. Having a car can be a problem. A car costs a lot to buy. There are many other expenses such as gas and repairs. Yet many people have cars. Do you think it is worth having the problems to own a car? Why or why not?

_____
_____
_____
_____

3 Put These Sentences in Order. Write these sentences in the correct time order on the lines below.

The policeman waited while Tony changed the tire.

Tony had a blowout as he drove.

Tony was only ten minutes late for his new job.

Tony thanked the policeman for keeping other cars from hitting him.

Tony drove his car to work.

Tony was fixing his flat tire when a police car stopped.

1. _____
_____

2. _____
_____

3. _____
_____

4. _____
_____

5. _____
_____

6. _____
_____

4 Write Paragraphs. Write short paragraphs using the questions below to guide you. Explain your answers.

1. What do you like to do for amusement?

    Do you like to go to the park, to the movies, to a ball game?

    Do you like to do things alone or with other people?

    Do you like to go places with friends or with family?

2. What kind of work do you like most?

Do you do that kind of work now?

Are you able to do that work?

What kind of training is needed for the work you like?

Where did you get training for this job, or where could you get the training?

If you don't do this work now, what must you do to get the job?

_____
_____
_____
_____
_____
_____
_____
_____
_____
_____
_____
_____
_____
_____
_____
_____
_____
_____
_____